american popular piano

2

ETUDES

Compositions by
Christopher Norton

Additional Compositions and Arrangements
Dr. Scott McBride Smith

Editor
Dr. Scott McBride Smith

Associate Editor
Clarke MacIntosh

Book Design & Engraving
Andrew Jones

Cover Design
Wagner Design

A Note about this Book

Pop music styles can be grouped into three broad categories:

- **lyrical** — pieces with a beautiful singing quality and rich harmonies; usually played at a slow tempo;

- **rhythmic** — more up-tempo pieces, with energetic, catchy rhythms; these often have a driving left hand part;

- **ensemble** — works meant to be played with other musicians, or with backing tracks (or both!); this type of piece requires careful listening and shared energy.

American Popular Piano has been deliberately designed to develop skills in all three areas.

You can integrate the cool, motivating pieces in **American Popular Piano** into your piano studies in several ways.

- pick a piece you like and learn it; when you're done, pick another!

- choose a piece from each category to develop a complete range of skills in your playing;

- polish a particular favorite for your local festival or competition. Works from **American Popular Piano** are featured on the lists of required pieces for many festivals and competitions;

- use the pieces as optional contemporary selections in music examinations;

- Or...just have fun!

Going hand-in-hand with the repertoire in **American Popular Piano** are the innovative **Etudes Albums** and **Skills Books**, designed to enhance each student's musical experience by building technical and aural skills.

- **Technical Etudes** in both Classical and Pop Styles are based on musical ideas and technical challenges drawn from the repertoire. Practice these to improve your chops!

- **Improvisation Etudes** offer an exciting new approach to improvisation that guides students effortlessly into spontaneous creativity. Not only does the user-friendly module structure integrate smoothly into traditional lessons, it opens up a whole new understanding of the repertoire being studied.

- **Skills Books** help students develop key supporting skills in sight-reading, ear-training and technic; presented in complementary study modules that are both practical and effective.

Use all of the elements of **American Popular Piano** together to incorporate a comprehensive course of study into your everyday routine. The carefully thought-out pacing makes learning almost effortless. Making music and real progress has never been so much fun!

Library and Archives Canada Cataloguing in Publication

Norton, Christopher, 1953-

American popular piano [music] : etudes / compositions by Christopher Norton ;
additional compositions and arrangements, Scott McBride Smith ;
editor, Scott McBride Smith ; associate editor, S. Clarke MacIntosh.

To be complete in 11 volumes.
The series is organized in 11 levels, from preparatory to level 10, each including a repertoire album,
an etudes album, a skills book, and an instrumental backings compact disc.

ISBN 1-897379-11-0 (preparatory level).--ISBN 1-897379-12-9 (level 1).--
ISBN 1-897379-13-7 (level 2).--ISBN 1-897379-14-5 (level 3).--
ISBN 1-897379-15-3 (level 4).--ISBN 1-897379-16-1 (level 5)

1. Piano--Studies and exercises. I. Smith, Scott McBride II. MacIntosh, S. Clarke, 1959- III. Title.

MT225.N883A52 2006 786.2 C2006906214-5

LEVEL 2 ETUDES
Table of Contents

Improv Etude - Toledo

MODULE 1

A Clap this rhythm: first *without*, then *with* the backing track.

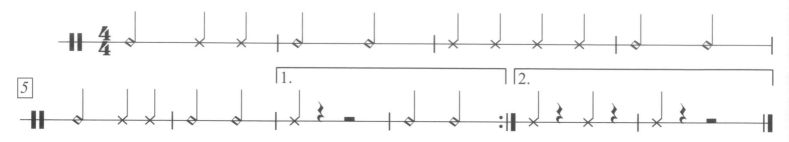

B Create your own RH melodies using the rhythm "A" above. The first few measures are done for you; you improvise the rest! Not every note will sound good with the backing track on steps 1 and 2. Listen closely and try with different notes on step 3.

1. Play the rhythm on one note:

etc.

2. Play the rhythm using two notes:

etc.

3. Improvise using 3, 4, or 5 notes:

etc.

C Learn a LH part to accompany your improv. Practice first *without* then *with* the backing track.

D Practice hands together. For mm.1-4, play as written; in mm. 5-8, improvise your own melodies using your ideas from step "B".

* Improv notes:

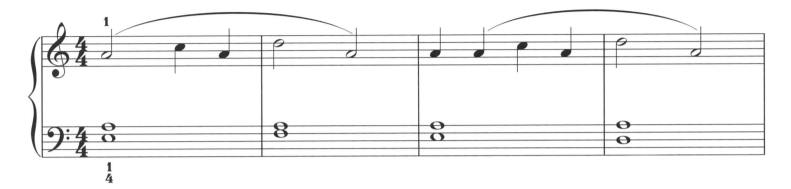

* IMPROVISATION:
use this rhythm

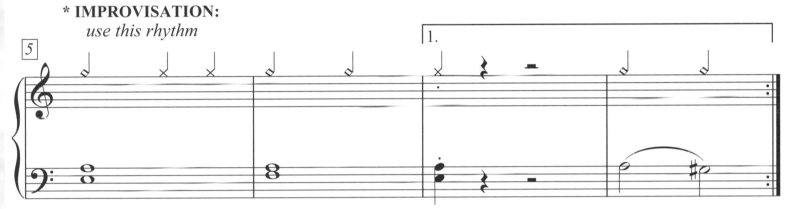

* use the Improv notes in any order.

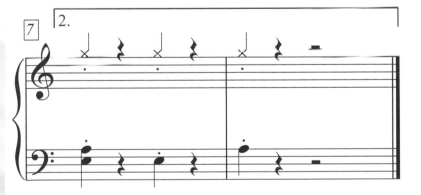

Listen closely as you play your improvisation.
- Does each note sound good with the backing track?
- Are you keeping a steady beat and staying with the backing track?
Play several different improvisations and choose your favorite. Play it for your teacher.

✔ **Improv Tip:** *Invent your own melodic motif (musical idea). You can keep it the same on the repeat or vary it.*

4

Improv Etude - Toledo

MODULE 2

A Clap this rhythm: first *without*, then *with* the backing track.

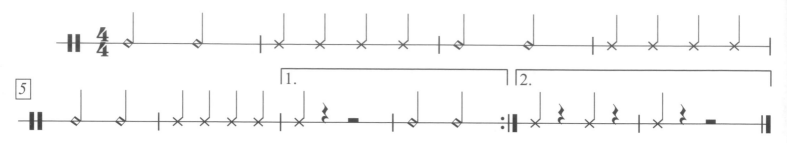

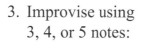

B Create your own RH melodies using the rhythm "A" above. The first few measures are done for you; you improvise the rest! Not every note will sound good with the backing track on steps 1 and 2. Listen closely and try with different notes on step 3.

1. Play the rhythm on one note:

2. Play the rhythm using two notes:

3. Improvise using 3, 4, or 5 notes:

C Learn a LH part to accompany your improv.
Practice first *without* then *with* the backing track.

D Practice hands together. For mm.1-4, play as written; in mm. 5-8, improvise your own melodies using your ideas from step "B".

* Improv notes:

* **IMPROVISATION:**
use this rhythm

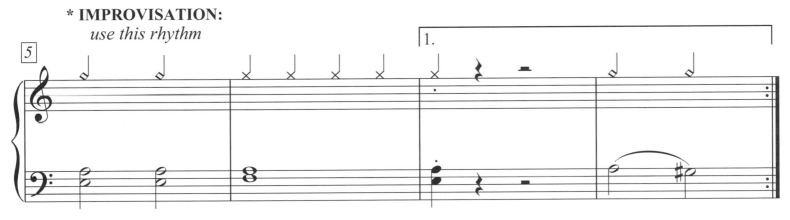

* use the Improv notes in any order.

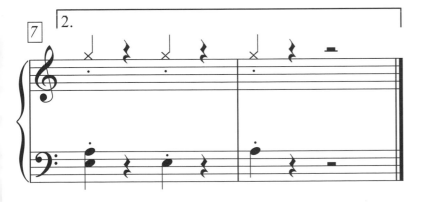

Listen closely as you play your improvisation.
- Does each note sound good with the backing track?
- Are you keeping a steady beat and staying with the backing track?

Play several different improvisations and choose your favorite. Play it for your teacher.

☑ **Improv Tip:** *Try playing your improvised melody up or down an octave on the repeat.*

Improv Etude - Toledo

MODULE 3

A Clap this rhythm: first *without*, then *with* the backing track.

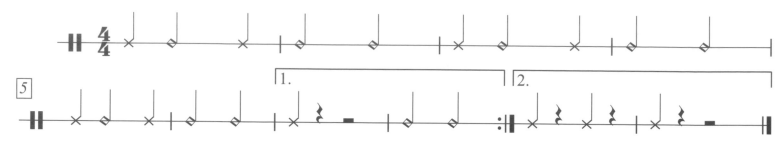

B Create your own RH melodies using the rhythm "A" above. The first few measures are done for you; you improvise the rest! Not every note will sound good with the backing track on steps 1 and 2. Listen closely and try with different notes on step 3.

1. Play the rhythm on one note:

2. Play the rhythm using two notes:

3. Improvise using 3, 4, or 5 notes:

C Learn a LH part to accompany your improv.
Practice first *without* then *with* the backing track.

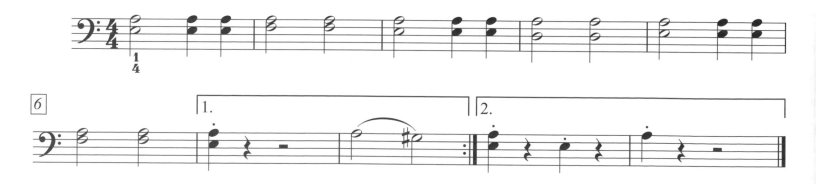

D Practice hands together. For mm.1-4, play as written; in mm. 5-8, improvise your own melodies using your ideas from step "B".

Improv notes:

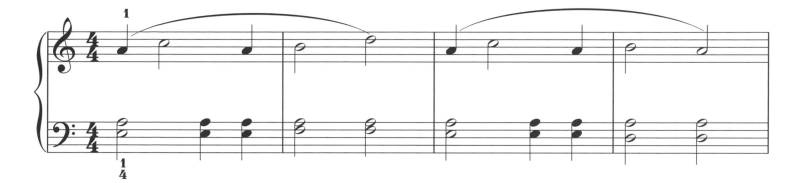

* IMPROVISATION:
use this rhythm

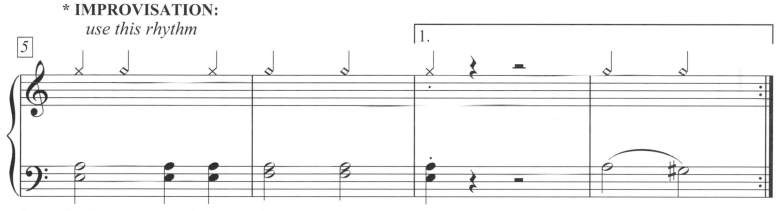

* use the Improv notes in any order.

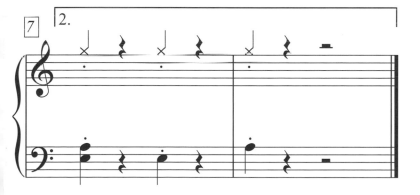

Listen closely as you play your improvisation.
  - Does each note sound good with the backing track?
  - Are you keeping a steady beat and staying with the backing track?
Play several different improvisations and choose your favorite. Play it for your teacher.

✔ **Improv Tip:**   *What intervals do you see in the melody in mm. 1-4? Try using the same ones in different combinations in your improvisation.*

Improv Etude - Toledo

MODULE 4

A Clap this rhythm: first *without*, then *with* the backing track.

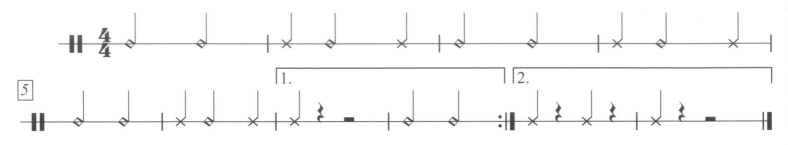

B Create your own RH melodies using the rhythm "A" above. The first few measures are done for you; you improvise the rest! Not every note will sound good with the backing track on steps 1 and 2. Listen closely and try with different notes on step 3.

1. Play the rhythm on one note:

2. Play the rhythm using two notes:

3. Improvise using 3, 4, or 5 notes:

C Learn a LH part to accompany your improv.
Practice first *without* then *with* the backing track.

D Practice hands together. For mm.1-4, play as written; in mm. 5-8, improvise your own melodies using your ideas from step "B".

* Improv notes:

* IMPROVISATION:
use this rhythm

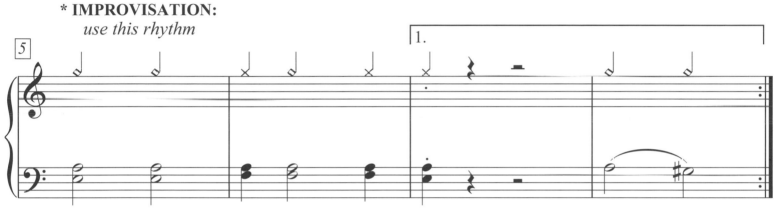

* use the Improv notes in any order.

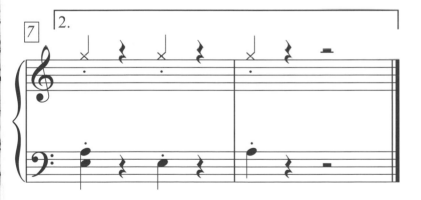

Listen closely as you play your improvisation.
 - Does each note sound good with the backing track?
 - Are you keeping a steady beat and staying with the backing track?
Play several different improvisations and choose your favorite. Play it for your teacher.

✔ Improv Tip: *Experiment with changing your improv melody notes on the repeat.*
Do all the Improv notes sound good in every measure?

Improv Etude - Freedom March

MODULE 1

A Clap this rhythm: first *without*, then *with* the backing track.

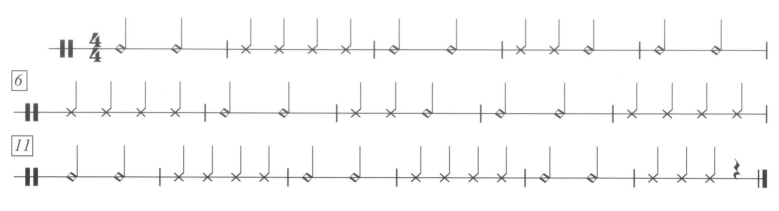

B Create your own RH melodies using the rhythm "A" above. The first few measures are done for you; you improvise the rest! Not every note will sound good with the backing track on steps 1 and 2. Listen closely and try with different notes on step 3.

1. Play the rhythm on one note:

etc.

2. Play the rhythm using two notes:

etc.

3. Improvise using 3, 4, or 5 notes:

etc.

C Learn a LH part to accompany your improv.
Practice first *without* then *with* the backing track.

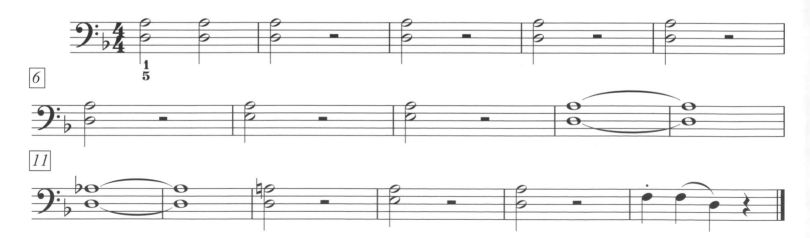

D Practice hands together. For mm.1-4, 9-12 & 16, play as written; in mm. 5-8 & 13-15, improvise your own melodies using your ideas from step "B".

* Improv notes:

* **IMPROVISATION:** *use this rhythm*

* use the Improv notes in any order.

Listen closely as you play your improvisation.
- Does each note sound good with the backing track?
- Are you keeping a steady beat and staying with the backing track?

Play several different improvisations and choose your favorite. Play it for your teacher.

✔ **Improv Tip:** *Playing different articulations is part of improvisation. Try varying your use of legato and staccato notes.*

Improv Etude - Freedom March

MODULE 2

A Clap this rhythm: first *without*, then *with* the backing track.

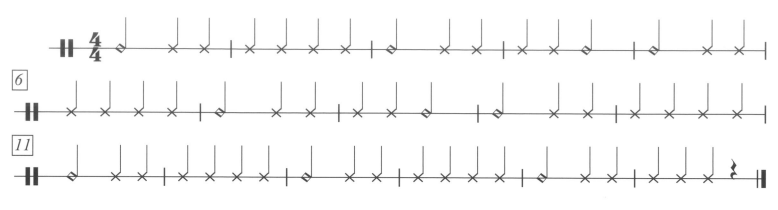

B Create your own RH melodies using the rhythm "A" above. The first few measures are done for you; you improvise the rest! Not every note will sound good with the backing track on steps 1 and 2. Listen closely and try with different notes on step 3.

1. Play the rhythm on one note:

2. Play the rhythm using two notes:

3. Improvise using 3, 4, or 5 notes:

C Learn a LH part to accompany your improv.
Practice first *without* then *with* the backing track.

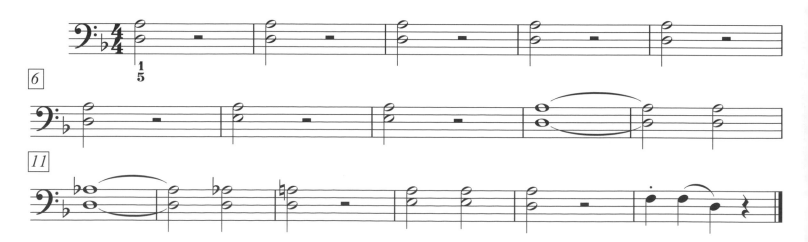

D Practice hands together. For mm.1-4, 9-12 & 16, play as written; in mm. 5-8 & 13-15, improvise your own melodies using your ideas from step "B".

* Improv notes:

* **IMPROVISATION:** *use this rhythm*

* use the Improv notes in any order.

Listen closely as you play your improvisation.
  - Does each note sound good with the backing track?
  - Are you keeping a steady beat and staying with the backing track?
Play several different improvisations and choose your favorite. Play it for your teacher.

✔ **Improv Tip:** *The simple left hand allows the right hand to play more notes.*
Experiment with using all of the Improv notes in a single improvisation.

Improv Etude - Freedom March

MODULE 3

A Clap this rhythm: first *without*, then *with* the backing track.

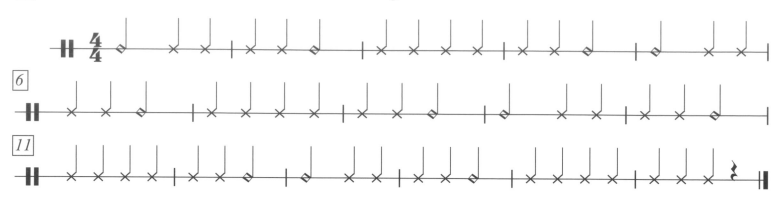

B Create your own RH melodies using the rhythm "A" above. The first few measures are done for you; you improvise the rest! Not every note will sound good with the backing track on steps 1 and 2. Listen closely and try with different notes on step 3.

1. Play the rhythm on one note:

etc.

2. Play the rhythm using two notes:

etc.

3. Improvise using 3, 4, or 5 notes:

etc.

C Learn a LH part to accompany your improv.
Practice first *without* then *with* the backing track.

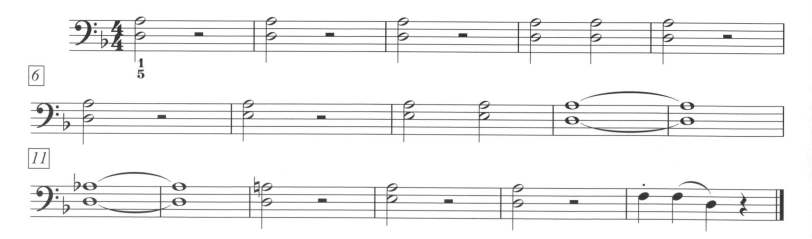

D Practice hands together. For mm.1-4, 9-12 & 16, play as written; in mm. 5-8 & 13-15, improvise your own melodies using your ideas from step "B".

* Improv notes:

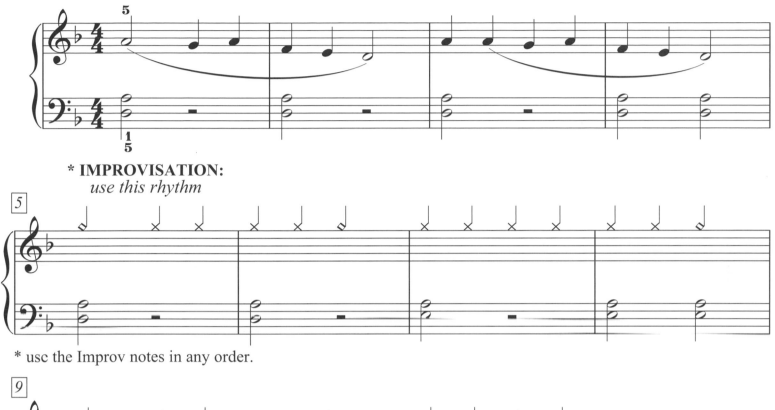

* IMPROVISATION:
use this rhythm

* use the Improv notes in any order.

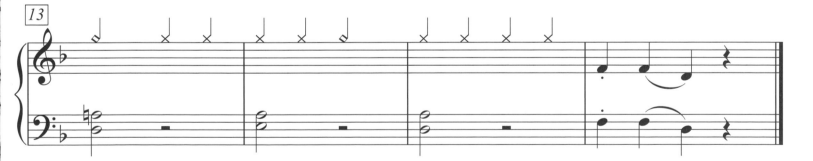

Listen closely as you play your improvisation.
- Does each note sound good with the backing track?
- Are you keeping a steady beat and staying with the backing track?
Play several different improvisations and choose your favorite. Play it for your teacher.

✔ **Improv Tip:** *mm. 5-8 could be a "question and answer". Try improvising mm. 5-6 so that you do **not** end up on D (a question) and mm. 7-8 so that you **do** end on D (an answer).*

Improv Etude - Freedom March

MODULE 4

A Clap this rhythm: first *without*, then *with* the backing track.

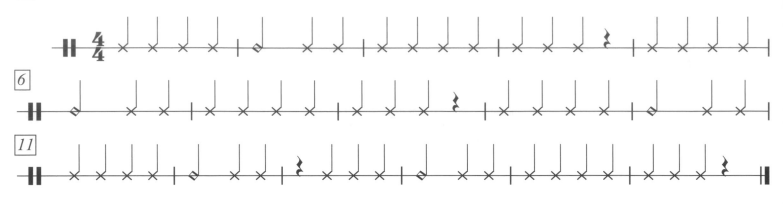

B Create your own RH melodies using the rhythm "A" above. The first few measures are done for you; you improvise the rest! Not every note will sound good with the backing track on steps 1 and 2. Listen closely and try with different notes on step 3.

1. Play the rhythm on one note:

2. Play the rhythm using two notes:

3. Improvise using 3, 4, or 5 notes:

C Learn a LH part to accompany your improv.
Practice first *without* then *with* the backing track.

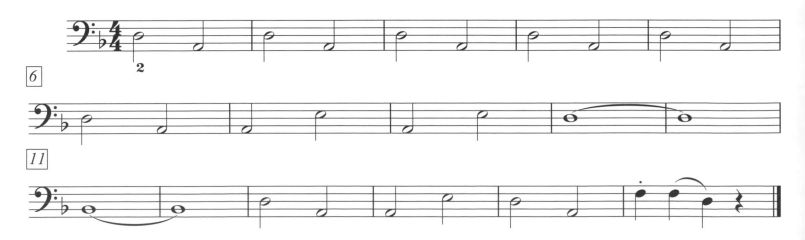

D Practice hands together. For mm.1-4, 9-12 & 16, play as written; in mm. 5-8 & 13-15, improvise your own melodies using your ideas from step "B".

* Improv notes:

* **IMPROVISATION:** *use this rhythm*

* use the Improv notes in any order.

Listen closely as you play your improvisation.
- Does each note sound good with the backing track?
- Are you keeping a steady beat and staying with the backing track?

Play several different improvisations and choose your favorite. Play it for your teacher.

✔ **Improv Tip:** *Measures 1-4 have a question and answer structure: mm. 1-2 are "answered" by mm. 3-4. Try this technique for your improvisation in mm. 5-8.*

Improv Etude - In Charge

MODULE 1

A Clap this rhythm: first *without*, then *with* the backing track.

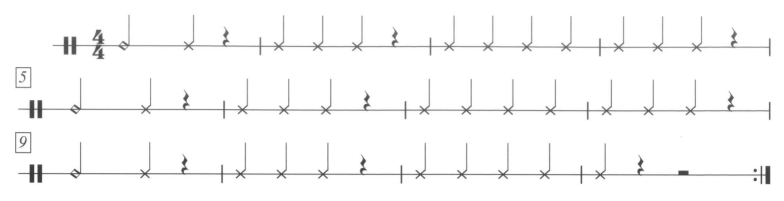

B Create your own RH melodies using the rhythm "A" above. The first few measures are done for you; you improvise the rest! Not every note will sound good with the backing track on steps 1 and 2. Listen closely and try with different notes on step 3.

1. Play the rhythm on one note:

etc.

2. Play the rhythm using two notes:

etc.

3. Improvise using 3 or 4 notes:

etc.

C Learn a LH part to accompany your improv.
Practice first *without* then *with* the backing track.

D Practice hands together. For mm.1-4 & 9-12, play as written; in mm. 5-8, improvise your own melodies using your ideas from step "B".

* Improv notes:

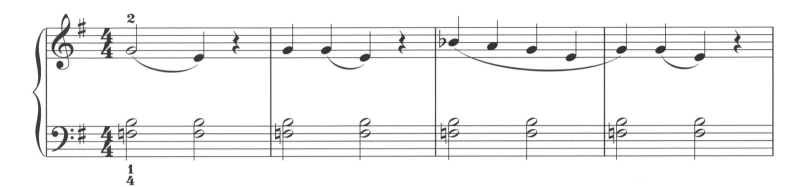

* **IMPROVISATION:**
use this rhythm

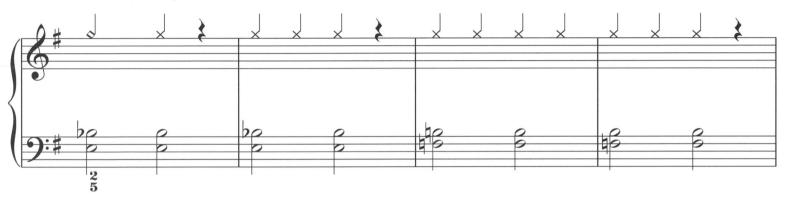

* use the Improv notes in any order.

Listen closely as you play your improvisation.
   - Does each note sound good with the backing track?
   - Are you keeping a steady beat and staying with the backing track?
Play several different improvisations and choose your favorite. Play it for your teacher.

✔ **Improv Tip:** *The B♭ is a 'blues' note - it sounds tangy against the B♮ in the left hand.*
        Try using it in your improvisation.

20

Improv Etude - In Charge

MODULE 2

A Clap this rhythm: first *without*, then *with* the backing track.

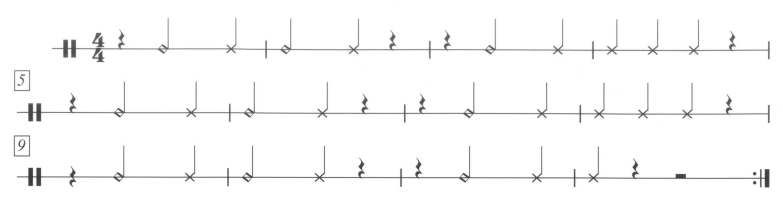

B Create your own RH melodies using the rhythm "A" above. The first few measures are done for you; you improvise the rest! Not every note will sound good with the backing track on steps 1 and 2. Listen closely and try with different notes on step 3.

1. Play the rhythm
   on one note:

2. Play the rhythm
   using two notes:

3. Improvise using
   3 or 4 notes:

C Learn a LH part to accompany your improv.
Practice first *without* then *with* the backing track.

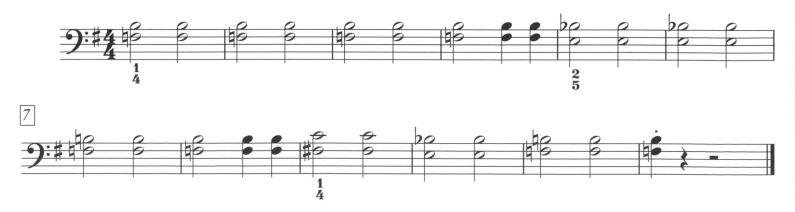

D Practice hands together. For mm.1-4 & 9-12, play as written; in mm. 5-8, improvise your own melodies using your ideas from step "B".

* Improv notes:

* IMPROVISATION:
use this rhythm

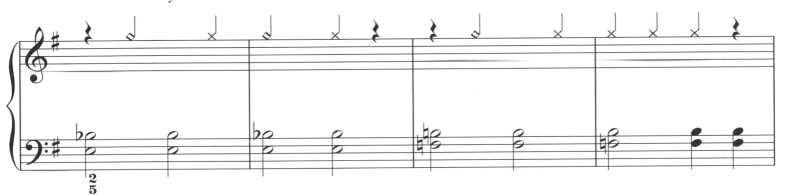

* use the Improv notes in any order.

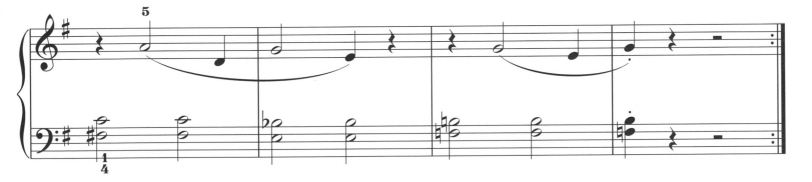

Listen closely as you play your improvisation.
- Does each note sound good with the backing track?
- Are you keeping a steady beat and staying with the backing track?
Play several different improvisations and choose your favorite. Play it for your teacher.

☑ **Improv Tip:** *Note the directions of the written melody. For example, the first measure goes down and the second goes up. Experiment with melodies that go in the opposite directions. This is known as contrary motion.*

Improv Etude - In Charge

MODULE 3

A Clap this rhythm: first *without*, then *with* the backing track.

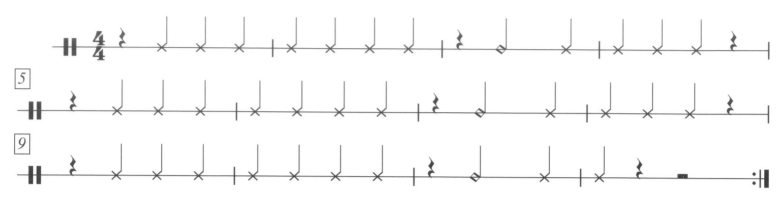

B Create your own RH melodies using the rhythm "A" above. The first few measures are done for you; you improvise the rest! Not every note will sound good with the backing track on steps 1 and 2. Listen closely and try with different notes on step 3.

1. Play the rhythm on one note:

2. Play the rhythm using two notes:

3. Improvise using 3 or 4 notes:

C Learn a LH part to accompany your improv.
Practice first *without* then *with* the backing track.

D Practice hands together. For mm.1-4 & 9-12, play as written; in mm. 5-8, improvise your own melodies using your ideas from step "B".

* Improv notes:

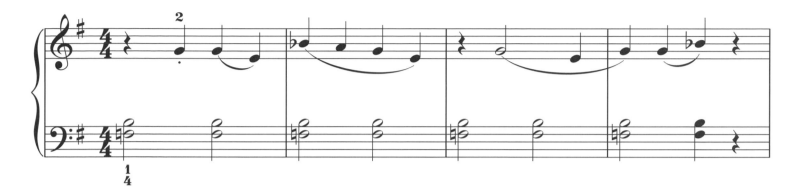

* IMPROVISATION:
use this rhythm

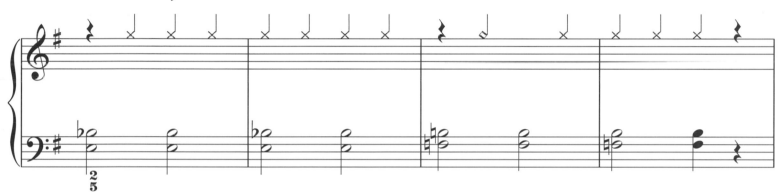

* use the Improv notes in any order.

Listen closely as you play your improvisation.
  - Does each note sound good with the backing track?
  - Are you keeping a steady beat and staying with the backing track?
Play several different improvisations and choose your favorite. Play it for your teacher.

☑ **Improv Tip:** *Notice how the written melodies use intervals of a second and a third. Use these in your improvisation, too.*

Improv Etude - In Charge

MODULE 4

A Clap this rhythm: first *without*, then *with* the backing track.

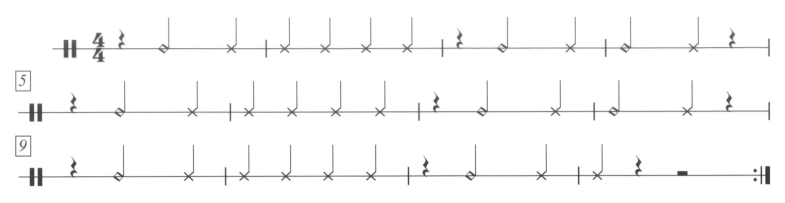

B Create your own RH melodies using the rhythm "A" above. The first few measures are done for you; you improvise the rest! Not every note will sound good with the backing track on steps 1 and 2. Listen closely and try with different notes on step 3.

1. Play the rhythm on one note:

2. Play the rhythm using two notes:

3. Improvise using 3 or 4 notes:

C Learn a LH part to accompany your improv.
Practice first *without* then *with* the backing track.

D Practice hands together. For mm.1-4 & 9-12, play as written; in mm. 5-8, improvise your own melodies using your ideas from step "B".

* Improv notes:

* IMPROVISATION:
use this rhythm

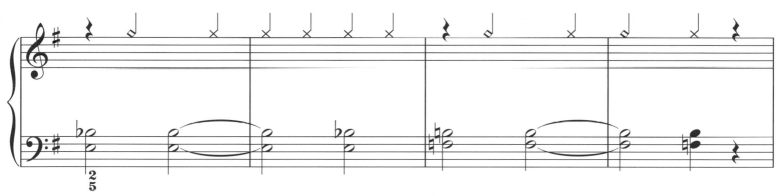

* use the Improv notes in any order.

Listen closely as you play your improvisation.
 - Does each note sound good with the backing track?
 - Are you keeping a steady beat and staying with the backing track?
Play several different improvisations and choose your favorite. Play it for your teacher.

✔ **Improv Tip:** *Try contrasting dynamics in your improvisation. Play the written parts louder and your improv softer - and vice versa!*

Improv Etude - Beach Walk

MODULE 1

A Clap this rhythm: first *without*, then *with* the backing track.

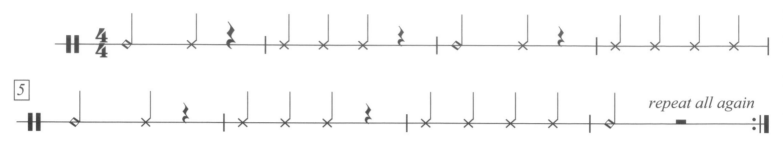

B Create your own RH melodies using the rhythm "A" above. The first few measures are done for you; you improvise the rest! Not every note will sound good with the backing track on steps 1 and 2. Listen closely and try with different notes on step 3.

1. Play the rhythm on one note:

2. Play the rhythm using two notes:

3. Improvise using up to six notes:

C Learn a LH part to accompany your improv.
Practice first *without* then *with* the backing track.

D Practice hands together. For mm.1-4, play
as written; in mm. 5-8, improvise your own
melodies using your ideas from step "B".

* Improv notes:

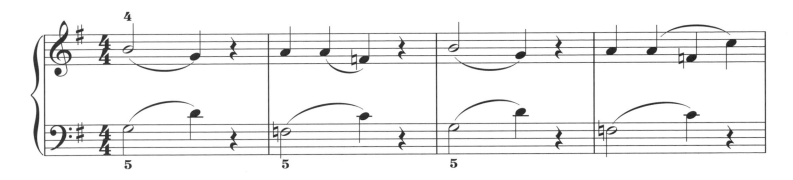

* IMPROVISATION:
use this rhythm

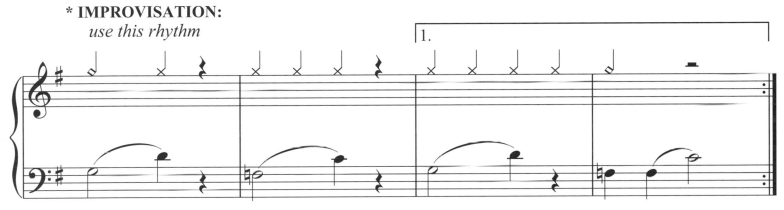

* use the Improv notes in any order.

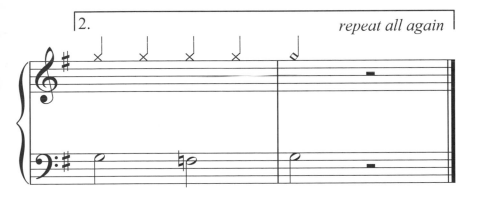

Listen closely as you play your improvisation.
- Does each note sound good with the backing track?
- Are you keeping a steady beat and staying with the backing track?
Play several different improvisations and choose your favorite. Play it for your teacher.

✔ **Improv Tip:** *This piece is in Mixolydian mode - like a G major scale with an F♮ instead of an F♯.*
You can use any note of the Mixolydian mode in your improvisation.

Improv Etude - Beach Walk

MODULE 2

A Clap this rhythm: first *without*, then *with* the backing track.

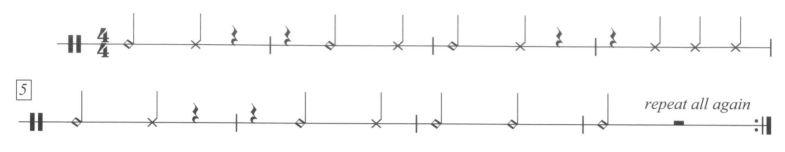

B Create your own RH melodies using the rhythm "A" above. The first few measures are done for you; you improvise the rest! Not every note will sound good with the backing track on steps 1 and 2. Listen closely and try with different notes on step 3.

1. Play the rhythm on one note:

2. Play the rhythm using two notes:

3. Improvise using up to six notes:

C Learn a LH part to accompany your improv.
Practice first *without* then *with* the backing track.

D Practice hands together. For mm.1-4, play
as written; in mm. 5-8, improvise your own
melodies using your ideas from step "B".

* Improv notes:

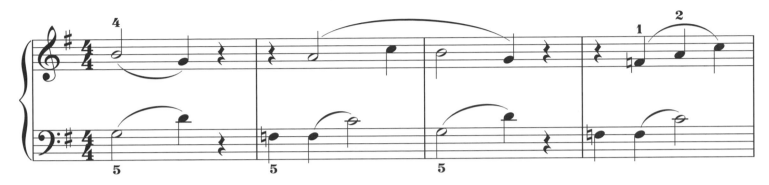

* IMPROVISATION:
use this rhythm

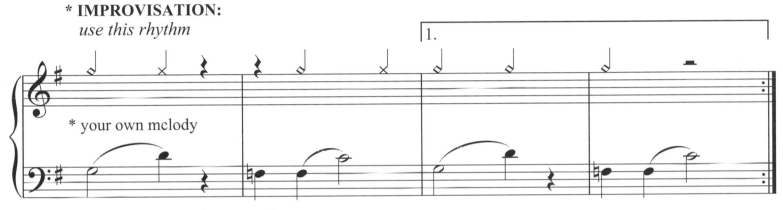

* your own mclody

* use the Improv notes in any order.

repeat all again

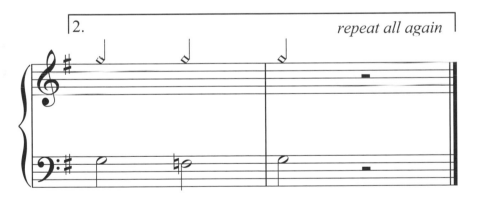

Listen closely as you play your improvisation.
 - Does each note sound good with the backing track?
 - Are you keeping a steady beat and staying with the backing track?
Play several different improvisations and choose your favorite. Play it for your teacher.

✔ **Improv Tip:** *Have you figured out what broken chord is used in each measure? Try adding passing
tones (notes that move by step, connecting chord tones) to your improvisation.*

Improv Etude - Beach Walk

A Clap this rhythm: first *without*, then *with* the backing track.

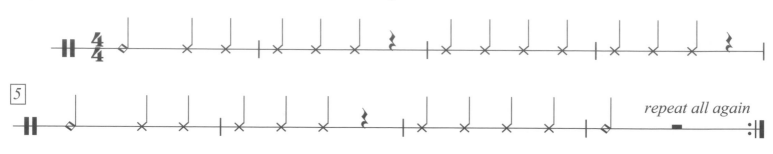

B Create your own RH melodies using the rhythm "A" above. The first few measures are done for you; you improvise the rest! Not every note will sound good with the backing track on steps 1 and 2. Listen closely and try with different notes on step 3.

1. Play the rhythm on one note:

2. Play the rhythm using two notes:

3. Improvise using up to six notes:

C Learn a LH part to accompany your improv.
Practice first *without* then *with* the backing track.

D Practice hands together. For mm.1-4, play
as written; in mm. 5-8, improvise your own
melodies using your ideas from step "B".

* Improv notes:

* IMPROVISATION:
use this rhythm

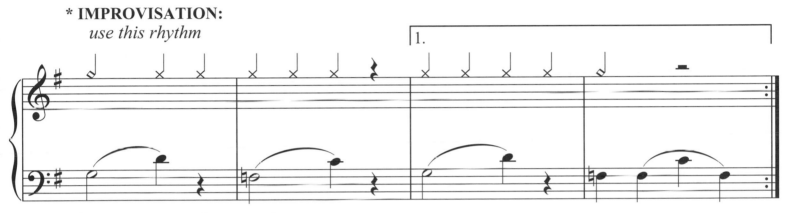

* use the Improv notes in any order.

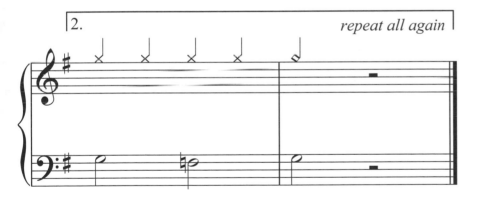

Listen closely as you play your improvisation.
- Does each note sound good with the backing track?
- Are you keeping a steady beat and staying with the backing track?
Play several different improvisations and choose your favorite. Play it for your teacher.

✔ **Improv Tip:** *There are a lot of repeated notes in mm. 1-4;*
try to use some in your improvisation.

Improv Etude - Beach Walk

MODULE 4

A Clap this rhythm: first *without*, then *with* the backing track.

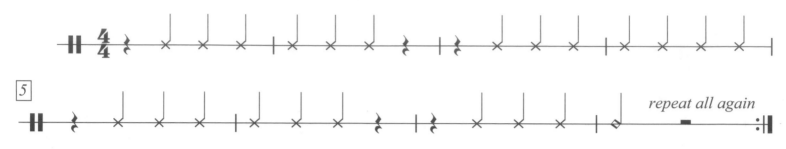

B Create your own RH melodies using the rhythm "A" above. The first few measures are done for you; you improvise the rest! Not every note will sound good with the backing track on steps 1 and 2. Listen closely and try with different notes on step 3.

1. Play the rhythm on one note:

2. Play the rhythm using two notes:

3. Improvise using up to six notes:

C Learn a LH part to accompany your improv.
Practice first *without* then *with* the backing track.

D Practice hands together. For mm.1-4, play as written; in mm. 5-8, improvise your own melodies using your ideas from step "B".

* Improv notes:

* IMPROVISATION:
use this rhythm

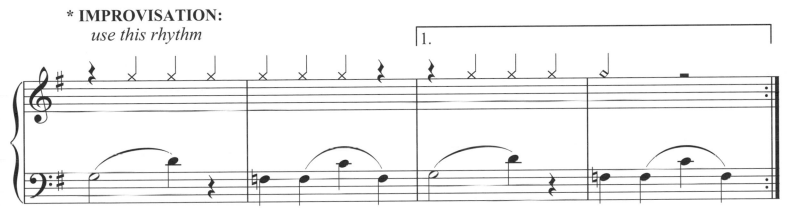

* use the Improv notes in any order.

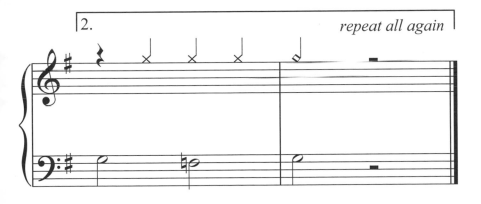

Listen closely as you play your improvisation.
  - Does each note sound good with the backing track?
  - Are you keeping a steady beat and staying with the backing track?
Play several different improvisations and choose your favorite. Play it for your teacher.

✔ **Improv Tip:** *Experiment with playing accents in different places.*
It will give the piece a different character.

Improv Etude - Howlin'

MODULE 1

A Clap this rhythm: first *without*, then *with* the backing track.

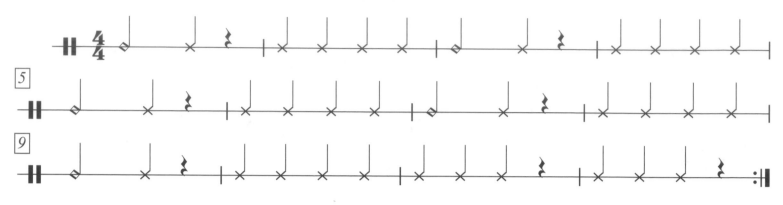

B Create your own RH melodies using the rhythm "A" above. The first few measures are done for you; you improvise the rest! Not every note will sound good with the backing track on steps 1 and 2. Listen closely and try with different notes on step 3.

1. Play the rhythm on one note:

2. Play the rhythm using two notes:

3. Improvise using up to six notes:

C Learn a LH part to accompany your improv.
Practice first *without* then *with* the backing track.

D Practice hands together. For mm.1-4 & 9-12, play as written; in mm. 5-8, improvise your own melodies using your ideas from step "B".

* Improv notes:

* IMPROVISATION:
use this rhythm

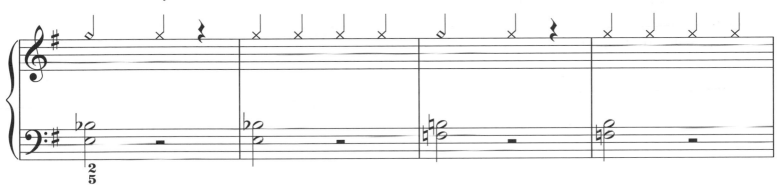

* use the Improv notes in any order.

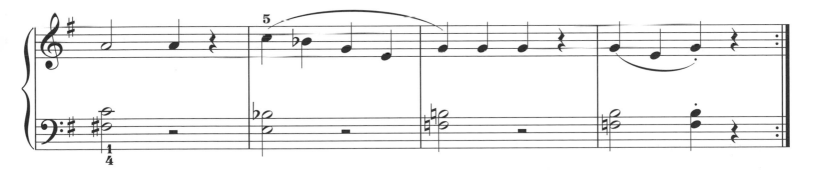

Listen closely as you play your improvisation.
  - Does each note sound good with the backing track?
  - Are you keeping a steady beat and staying with the backing track?
Play several different improvisations and choose your favorite. Play it for your teacher.

✔ **Improv Tip:** *Don't forget about blues notes! Use the B♭ in the Improv Notes to give your improvisation a 'bluesy' feel. You may have to write in some fingering.*

Improv Etude - Howlin'

36

MODULE 2

A Clap this rhythm: first *without*, then *with* the backing track.

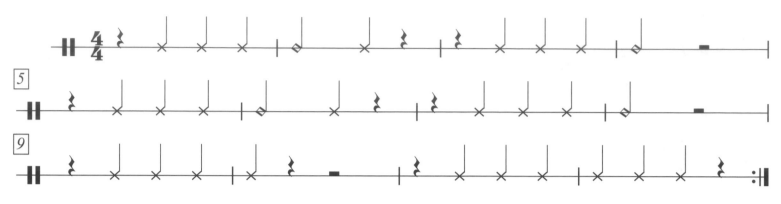

B Create your own RH melodies using the rhythm "A" above. The first few measures are done for you; you improvise the rest! Not every note will sound good with the backing track on steps 1 and 2. Listen closely and try with different notes on step 3.

1. Play the rhythm on one note:

2. Play the rhythm using two notes:

3. Improvise using up to six notes:

C Learn a LH part to accompany your improv.
Practice first *without* then *with* the backing track.

D Practice hands together. For mm.1-4 & 9-12, play as written; in mm. 5-8, improvise your own melodies using your ideas from step "B".

* Improv notes:

* IMPROVISATION:
use this rhythm

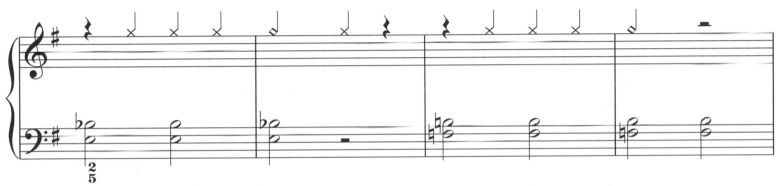

* use the Improv notes in any order.

Listen closely as you play your improvisation.
 - Does each note sound good with the backing track?
 - Are you keeping a steady beat and staying with the backing track?
Play several different improvisations and choose your favorite. Play it for your teacher.

✔ **Improv Tip:** *Try changing the written melody (mm. 1-4) by only one note in mm. 5-8.*

Improv Etude - Howlin'

MODULE 3

A Clap this rhythm: first *without*, then *with* the backing track.

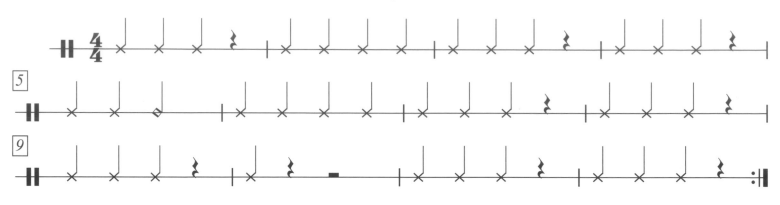

B Create your own RH melodies using the rhythm "A" above. The first few measures are done for you; you improvise the rest! Not every note will sound good with the backing track on steps 1 and 2. Listen closely and try with different notes on step 3.

1. Play the rhythm on one note:

2. Play the rhythm using two notes:

3. Improvise using up to six notes:

C Learn a LH part to accompany your improv.
Practice first *without* then *with* the backing track.

D Practice hands together. For mm.1-4 & 9-12, play as written; in mm. 5-8, improvise your own melodies using your ideas from step "B".

* Improv notes:

* IMPROVISATION:
use this rhythm

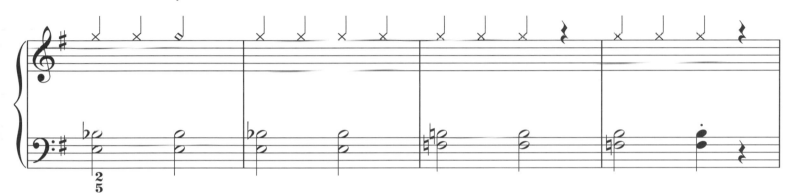

* use the Improv notes in any order.

Listen closely as you play your improvisation.
  - Does each note sound good with the backing track?
  - Are you keeping a steady beat and staying with the backing track?
Play several different improvisations and choose your favorite. Play it for your teacher.

✔ **Improv Tip:** *What interval do you find most often in the melody in mm. 1-4? Try adding some passing tones (steps moving stepwise that connect chord tones) in your improvisation.*

Improv Etude - Howlin'

MODULE 4

A Clap this rhythm: first *without*, then *with* the backing track.

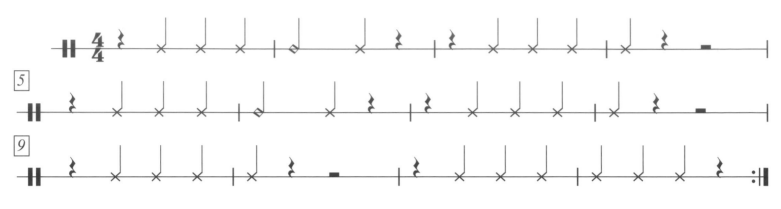

B Create your own RH melodies using the rhythm "A" above. The first few measures are done for you; you improvise the rest! Not every note will sound good with the backing track on steps 1 and 2. Listen closely and try with different notes on step 3.

1. Play the rhythm on one note:

etc.

2. Play the rhythm using two notes:

etc.

3. Improvise using up to six notes:

etc.

C Learn a LH part to accompany your improv.
Practice first *without* then *with* the backing track.

D Practice hands together. For mm.1-4 & 9-12, play as written; in mm. 5-8, improvise your own melodies using your ideas from step "B".

* Improv notes:

* IMPROVISATION:
use this rhythm

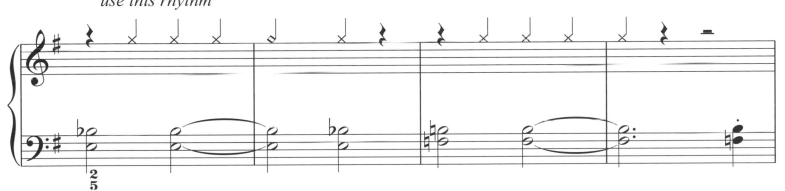

* use the Improv notes in any order.

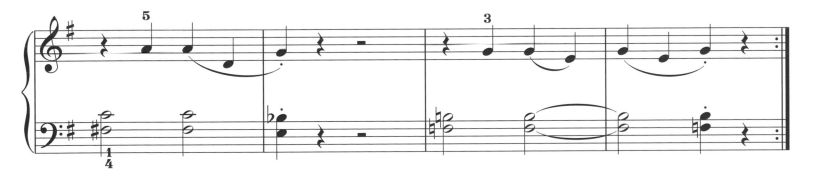

Listen closely as you play your improvisation.
- Does each note sound good with the backing track?
- Are you keeping a steady beat and staying with the backing track?

Play several different improvisations and choose your favorite. Play it for your teacher.

☑ **Improv Tip:** *Try substituting other chord tones for repeated notes when you improvise.*

Improv Etude - Breaking Rocks

MODULE 1

A Clap this rhythm: first *without*, then *with* the backing track.

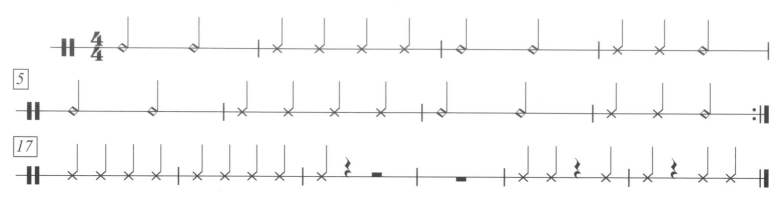

B Create your own RH melodies using the rhythm "A" above. The first few measures are done for you; you improvise the rest! Not every note will sound good with the backing track on steps 1 and 2. Listen closely and try with different notes on step 3.

1. Play the rhythm on one note:

2. Play the rhythm using two notes:

3. Improvise using 3, 4, or 5 notes:

C Learn a LH part to accompany your improv.
Practice first *without* then *with* the backing track.

D Practice hands together. For mm.1-4, 9-12 & 17-22, play as written; in mm. 5-8 & 13-16, improvise your own melodies using your ideas from step "B".

* Improv notes:

use this rhythm

* **IMPROVISATION:**

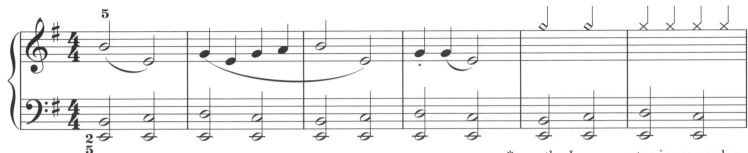

* use the Improv notes in any order.

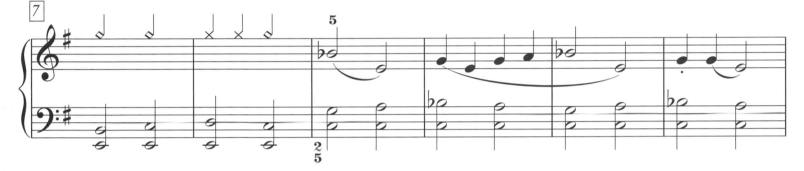

* **IMPROVISATION:** *use this rhythm*

* use the Improv notes in any order.

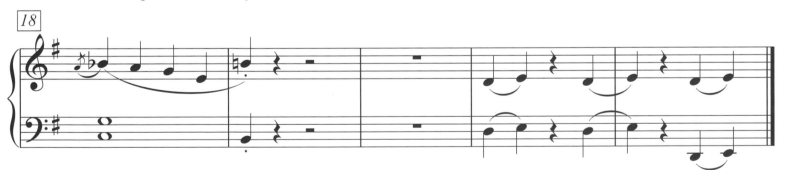

Listen closely as you play your improvisation.
- Does each note sound good with the backing track?
- Are you keeping a steady beat and staying with the backing track?

Play several different improvisations and choose your favorite. Play it for your teacher.

✔ **Improv Tip:** *Here's another 'blues' note, this time in the key of e minor.*
Experiment with using both B♭ and B♮ in your improvisation.

Improv Etude - Breaking Rocks

MODULE 2

A Clap this rhythm: first *without*, then *with* the backing track.

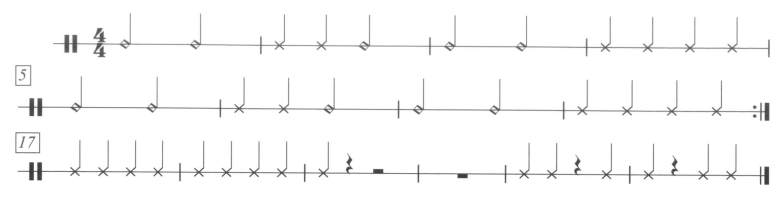

B Create your own RH melodies using the rhythm "A" above. The first few measures are done for you; you improvise the rest! Not every note will sound good with the backing track on steps 1 and 2. Listen closely and try with different notes on step 3.

1. Play the rhythm on one note:

2. Play the rhythm using two notes:

3. Improvise using 3, 4, or 5 notes:

C Learn a LH part to accompany your improv.
Practice first *without* then *with* the backing track.

D Practice hands together. For mm.1-4, 9-12 & 17-22, play as written; in mm. 5-8 & 13-16, improvise your own melodies using your ideas from step "B".

* Improv notes:

use this
* **IMPROVISATION:** *rhythm*

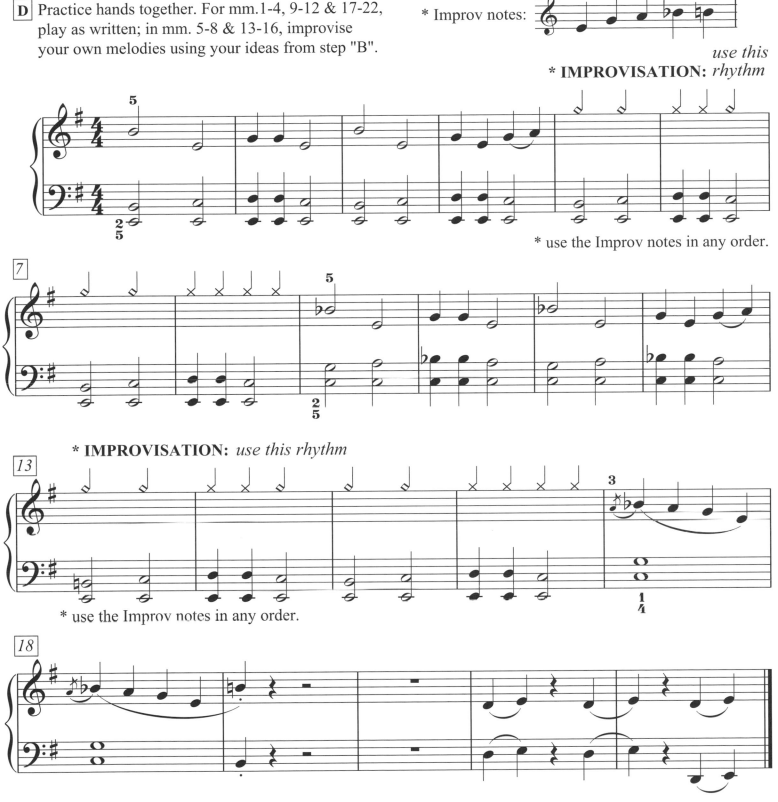

* use the Improv notes in any order.

* **IMPROVISATION:** *use this rhythm*

* use the Improv notes in any order.

Listen closely as you play your improvisation.
- Does each note sound good with the backing track?
- Are you keeping a steady beat and staying with the backing track?
Play several different improvisations and choose your favorite. Play it for your teacher.

✔ **Improv Tip:** *Variation is a great idea for an improvisation!*
Try repeating your melodic idea and then change only a couple of notes.

Improv Etude - Breaking Rocks

MODULE 3

A   Clap this rhythm: first *without*, then *with* the backing track.

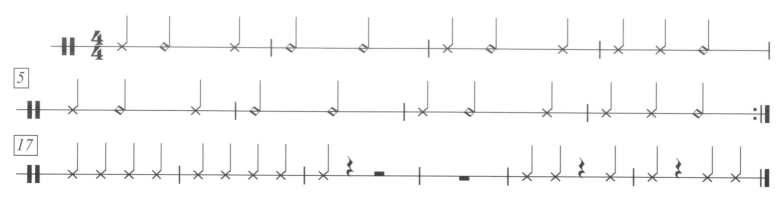

B   Create your own RH melodies using the rhythm "A" above. The first few measures are done for you; you improvise the rest! Not every note will sound good with the backing track on steps 1 and 2. Listen closely and try with different notes on step 3.

1. Play the rhythm on one note: *etc.*

2. Play the rhythm using two notes: *etc.*

3. Improvise using 3, 4, or 5 notes: *etc.*

C   Learn a LH part to accompany your improv.
Practice first *without* then *with* the backing track.

D Practice hands together. For mm.1-4, 9-12 & 17-22, play as written; in mm. 5-8 & 13-16, improvise your own melodies using your ideas from step "B".

* Improv notes:

use this rhythm

* **IMPROVISATION:**

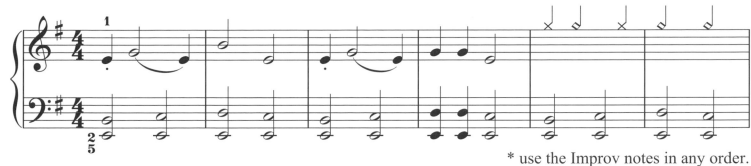

* use the Improv notes in any order.

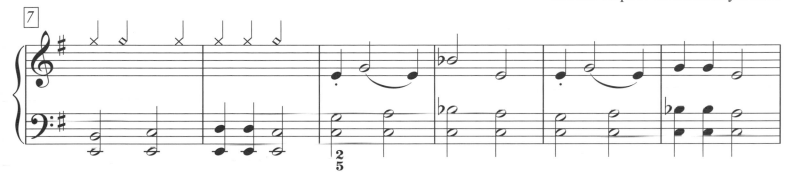

* **IMPROVISATION:** *use this rhythm*

* use the Improv notes in any order.

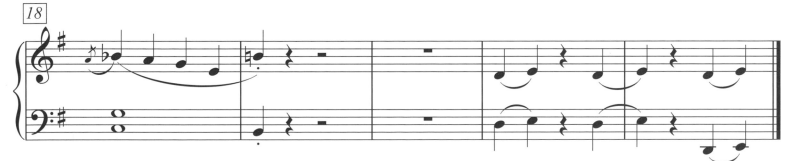

Listen closely as you play your improvisation.
- Does each note sound good with the backing track?
- Are you keeping a steady beat and staying with the backing track?

Play several different improvisations and choose your favorite. Play it for your teacher.

✔ **Improv Tip:** *The written melody has many intervals of a third and a fifth. Use these in your improvisation, too.*

Improv Etude - Breaking Rocks

MODULE 4

A Clap this rhythm: first *without*, then *with* the backing track.

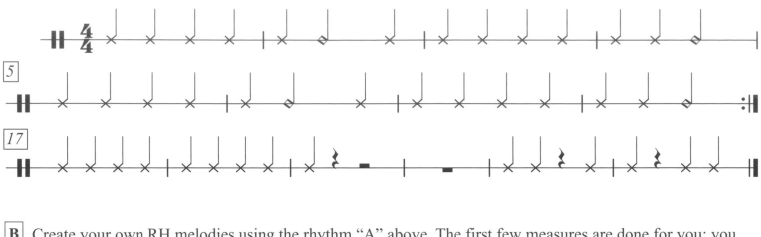

B Create your own RH melodies using the rhythm "A" above. The first few measures are done for you; you improvise the rest! Not every note will sound good with the backing track on steps 1 and 2. Listen closely and try with different notes on step 3.

1. Play the rhythm on one note:

etc.

2. Play the rhythm using two notes:

etc.

3. Improvise using 3, 4, or 5 notes:

etc.

C Learn a LH part to accompany your improv.
Practice first *without* then *with* the backing track.

D Practice hands together. For mm.1-4, 9-12 & 17-22, play as written; in mm. 5-8 & 13-16, improvise your own melodies using your ideas from step "B".

* Improv notes:

use this
* **IMPROVISATION:** *rhythm*

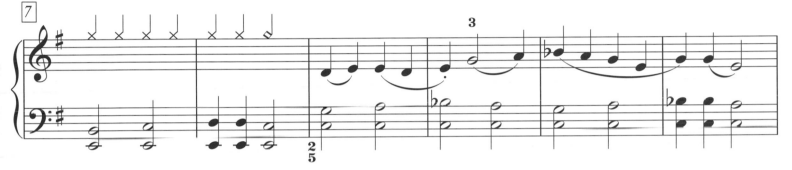

* use the Improv notes in any order.

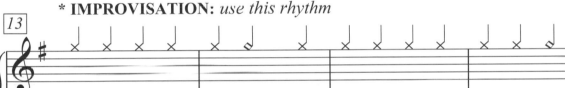

* **IMPROVISATION:** *use this rhythm*

* use the Improv notes in any order.

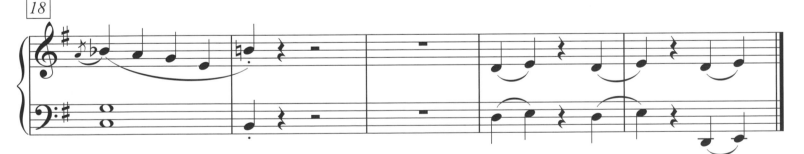

Listen closely as you play your improvisation.
- Does each note sound good with the backing track?
- Are you keeping a steady beat and staying with the backing track?
Play several different improvisations and choose your favorite. Play it for your teacher.

✔ **Improv Tip:** *For your improvisation, try playing some of the motifs (musical ideas) from mm. 1-4 in a different order in mm. 5-8.*

Performance Etude - Toledo

A Practice the *Toledo* Performance Etude based on
the notes and rhythms you have already used in the modules.
Once this feels comfortable, experiment with your own rhythms.
Do this several times.

Improv notes:

B Work on your improvisation without the backing track until you can play with a steady tempo.
Then practice with the backing track. Choose your favorite version and play it for your teacher.

Listen closely as you play your improvisation.
- Does each note sound good with the backing track?
- Are you keeping a steady beat and staying with the backing track?

✔ Improv Tip: *Play an idea loudly, then answer it quietly (an echo).*

Performance Etude - Freedom March

A Practice the *Freedom March* Performance Etude based on
the notes and rhythms you have already used in the modules.
Once this feels comfortable, experiment with your own rhythms.
Do this several times.

Improv notes:

B Work on your improvisation without the backing track until you can play with a steady tempo.
Then practice with the backing track. Choose your favorite version and play it for your teacher.

Listen closely as you play your improvisation.
- Does each note sound good with the backing track?
- Are you keeping a steady beat and staying with the backing track?

✔ **Improv Tip:** *You can vary "questions and answers" by adding extra repeated notes - or taking them out!*

Performance Etude - In Charge

A Practice the *Getting Closer* Performance Etude based on
the notes and rhythms you have already used in the modules.
Once this feels comfortable, experiment with your own rhythms.
Do this several times.

Improv notes:

B Work on your improvisation without the backing track until you can play with a steady tempo.
Then practice with the backing track. Choose your favorite version and play it for your teacher.

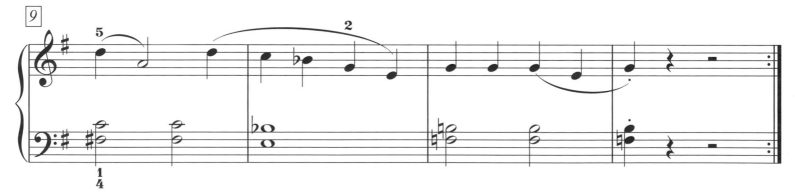

Listen closely as you play your improvisation.
- Does each note sound good with the backing track?
- Are you keeping a steady beat and staying with the backing track?

✔ **Improv Tip:** *You can play a small variation on the given melody.*
Try changing just one note.

Performance Etude - Beach Walk

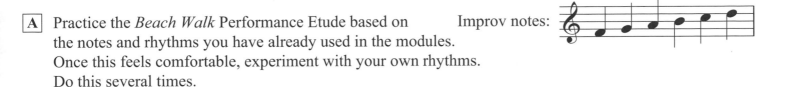

A Practice the *Beach Walk* Performance Etude based on
the notes and rhythms you have already used in the modules.
Once this feels comfortable, experiment with your own rhythms.
Do this several times.

Improv notes:

B Work on your improvisation without the backing track until you can play with a steady tempo.
Then practice with the backing track. Choose your favorite version and play it for your teacher.

Listen closely as you play your improvisation.
- Does each note sound good with the backing track?
- Are you keeping a steady beat and staying with the backing track?

✔ **Improv Tip:** *Keep your ideas simple and clear -
the left hand pattern makes it hard to do complicated things.*

Performance Etude - Howlin'

A Practice the *Howlin'* Performance Etude based on
the notes and rhythms you have already used in the modules.
Once this feels comfortable, experiment with your own rhythms.
Do this several times.

Improv notes:

B Work on your improvisation without the backing track until you can play with a steady tempo.
Then practice with the backing track. Choose your favorite version and play it for your teacher.

Listen closely as you play your improvisation.
- Does each note sound good with the backing track?
- Are you keeping a steady beat and staying with the backing track?

✔ **Improv Tip:** *When one hand has a complicated rhythm, it's a good idea to keep the other part simpler.*

Performance Etude - Breaking Rocks

A Practice the *Breaking Rocks* Performance Etude based on the notes and rhythms you have already used in the modules. Once this feels comfortable, experiment with your own rhythms. Do this several times.

Improv notes: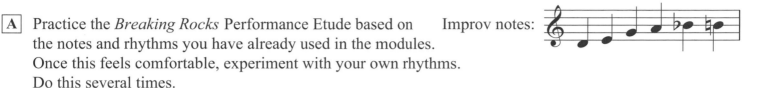

B Work on your improvisation without the backing track until you can play with a steady tempo. Then practice with the backing track. Choose your favorite version and play it for your teacher.

Listen closely as you play your improvisation.
- Does each note sound good with the backing track?
- Are you keeping a steady beat and staying with the backing track?

✔ **Improv Tip:** *Analyze the broken chord in each measure. You can use the chord tones in any order you like!*

After Beyer

Scott McBride Smith

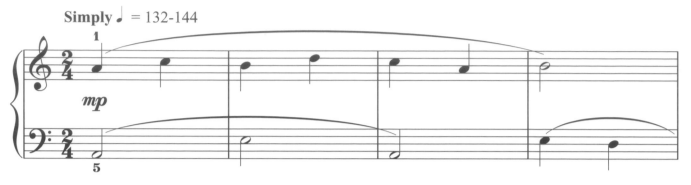

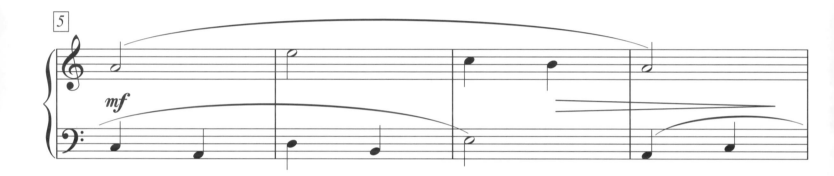

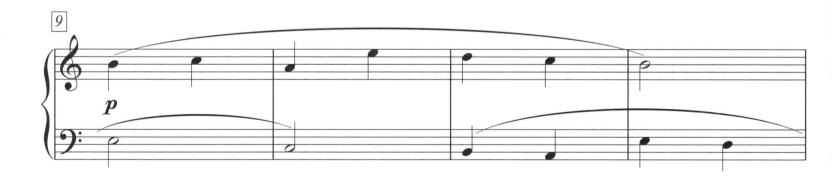

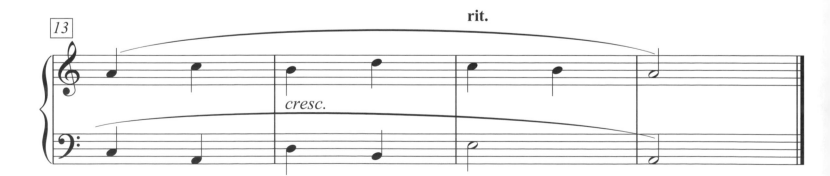

After Wayfaring Stranger

Scott McBride Smith

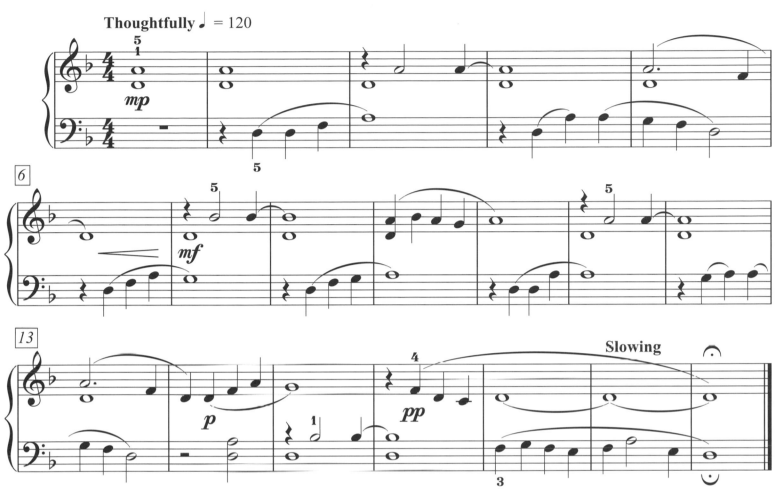

After Bartok

Scott McBride Smith

After Kohler

Scott McBride Smith

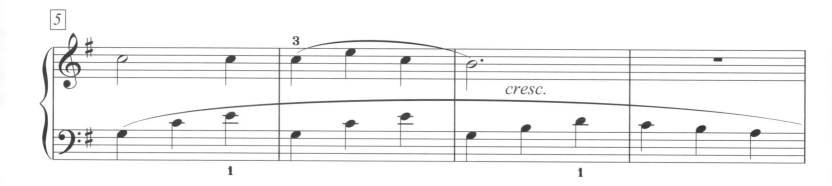

After Czerny no.1

Scott McBride Smith

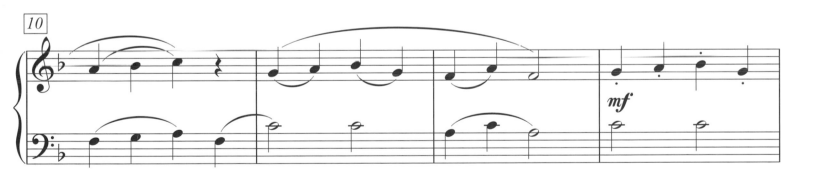

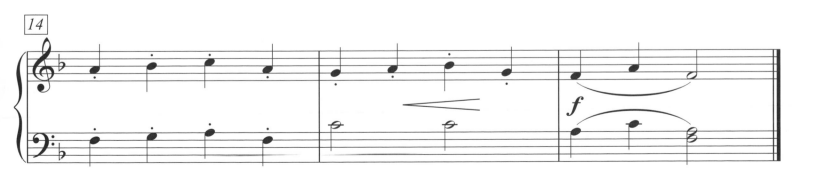

After Berens

Scott McBride Smith

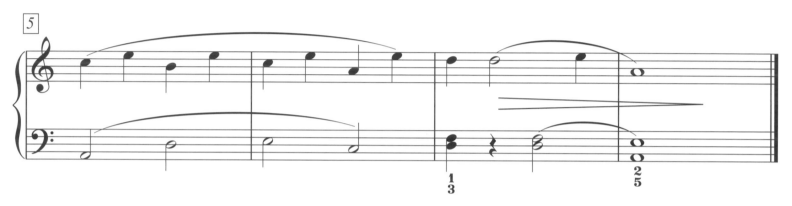

After Burgmüller

Scott McBride Smith

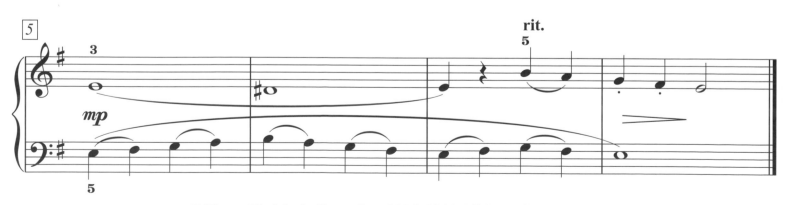

After Czerny no.2

Scott McBride Smith

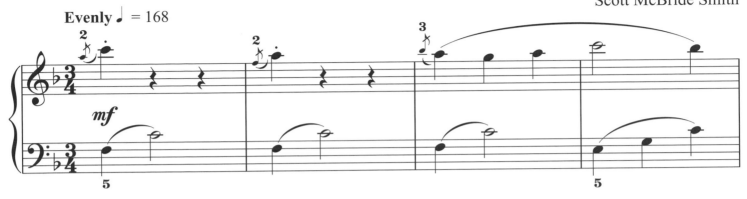

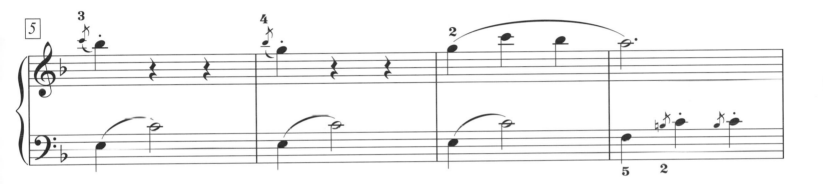

After Schytte

Scott McBride Smith

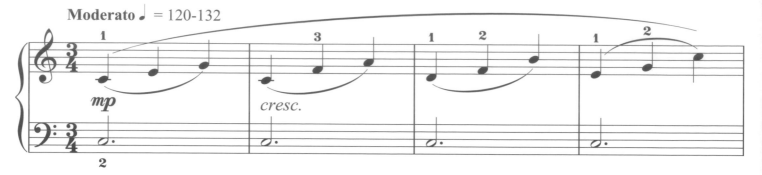

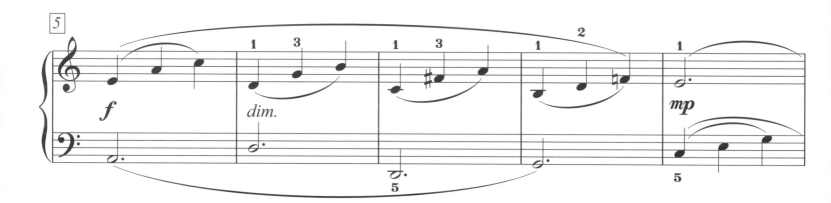

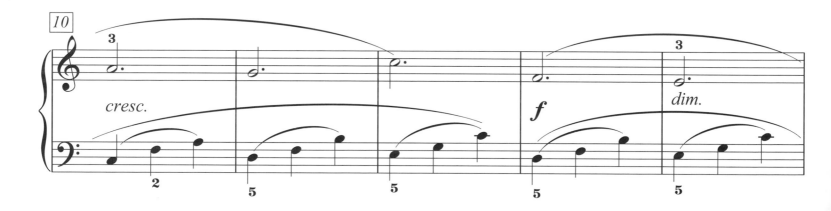

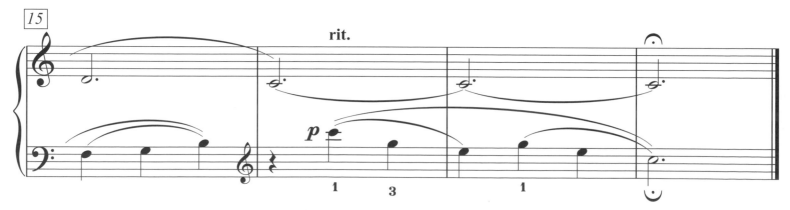

Country Outing

Christopher Norton

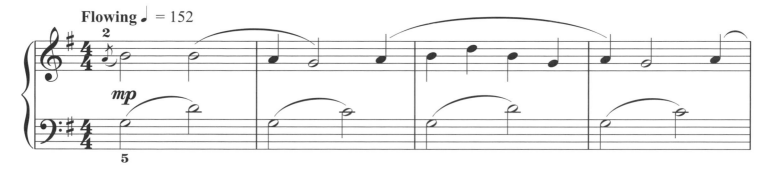

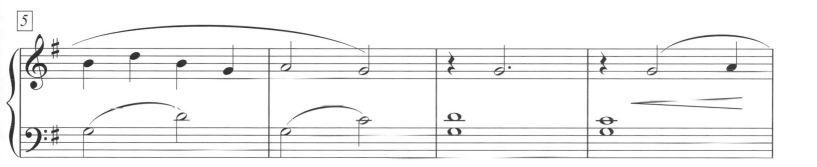

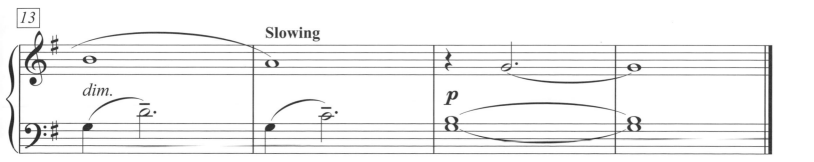

64

In The Distance

Christopher Norton

Exercise Yard

Christopher Norton

Lonesome

Christopher Norton

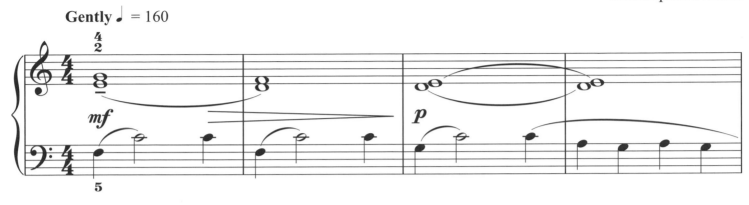

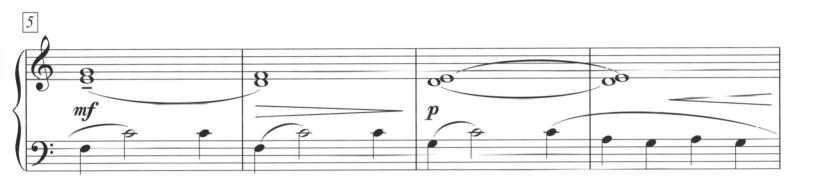

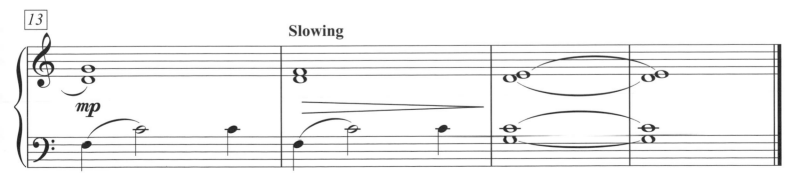

Calm Day

Christopher Norton

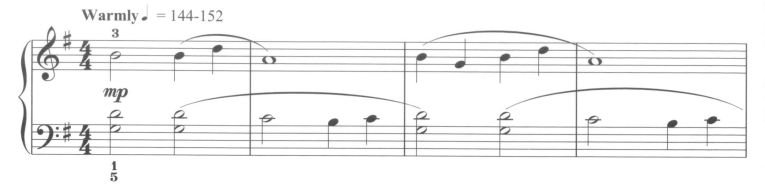

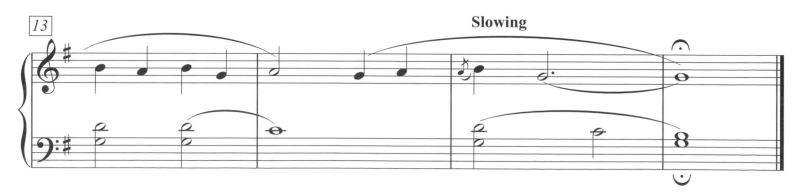

Getting Dynamic

Christopher Norton

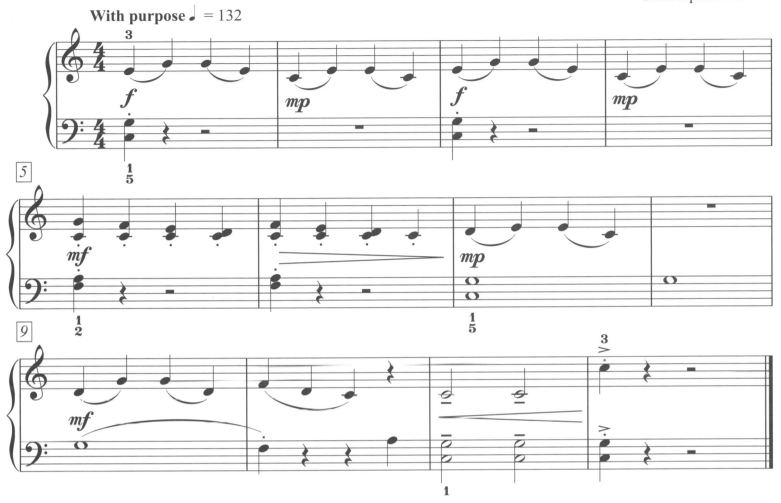

Oscillations

Christopher Norton

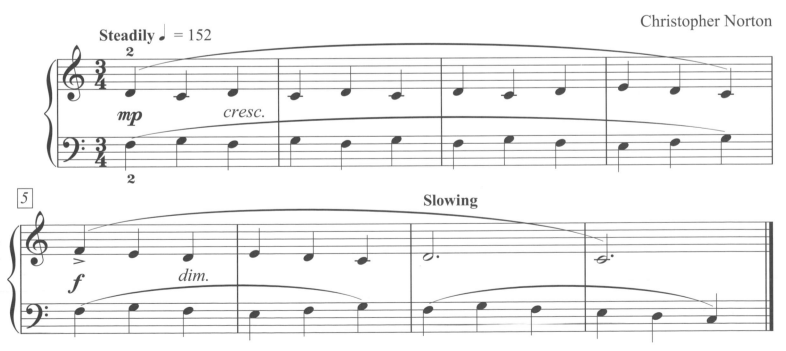

Battle Plan

Christopher Norton

Daytime Dreaming

Christopher Norton

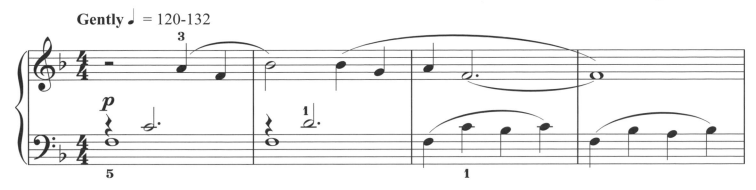

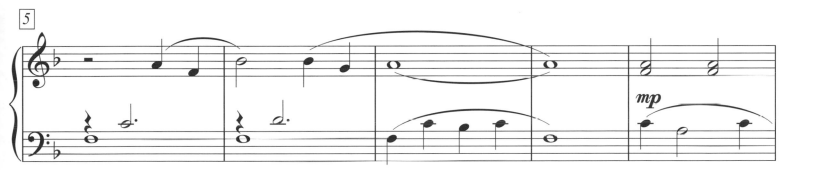

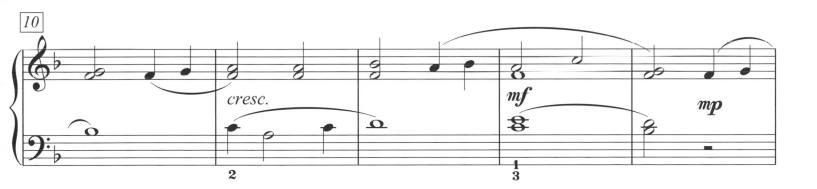

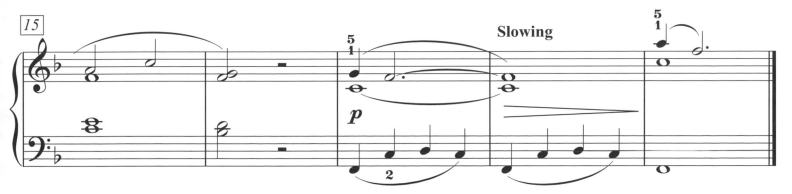

LEVEL 2 ETUDES

Improv Ideas

Toledo

Freedom March

In Charge

Beach Walk

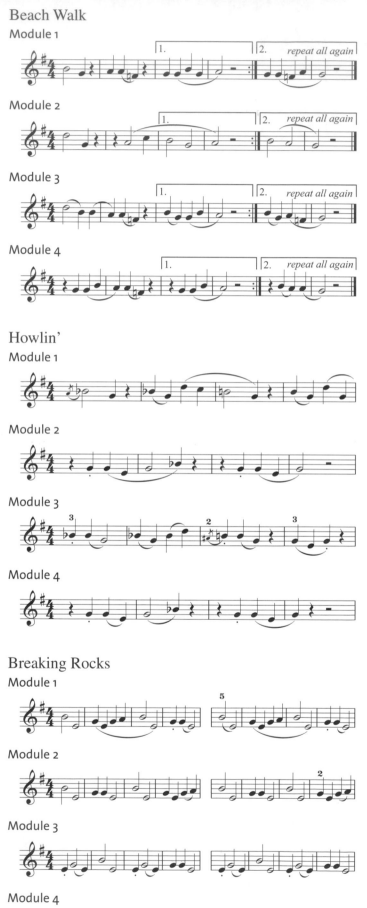

Howlin'

Breaking Rocks